One Fish from the Rooftop

One Fish from the Rooftop

poems
by

John Mikhail Asfour

Cormorant Books

Copyright © John Mikhail Asfour

Published with the assistance of the Canada Council,
the Ontario Arts Council, and the Secretary of State
for Multiculturalism. The support of the Government
of Ontario through the Ministry of Culture and
Communications is acknowledged.

The cover is from a hand-tinted lithograph, *The Sailor,*
(56.5 x 76 cm. 1978) by Kelly Clark,
courtesy of the artist and the Canada Council Art Bank.

Published by Cormorant Books, RR 1, Dunvegan,
Ontario, Canada K0C 1J0.

Printed and bound in Canada.

Canadian Cataloguing in Publication Data

    Asfour, John, 1945-

        One fish from the rooftop

    ISBN 0-920953-84-0

        I. Title.

PS8551.S36064 1992   C811'.54   C92-090455-6
PR9199.3.A84064 1992

*To Alison, Jonathan and Mikaela
with love*

TABLE OF CONTENTS

Off the Map	9
On the Other Shore	11
Made in Heaven	12
Breach of Promise	14
A Kiss	15
A Lullaby	16
Zero Hour	18
Not in the Books	19
Enemy Ears	21
One Could Do Worse	22
Through a Glass	24
Ben Hilali's Night of Revels	27
A Native Son Remembers Us in His Will	35
Inventory	37
In Suspense	38
An Umbrella	40
The Cocktail Hour	41
Innocent Pursuits	42
Ancestral Voices	45
We Have Some Sight Left	46
R.I.P.	51
The Contortionist	52
Words	53
One Fish	54
Fortunes	56
All the Lights	57
The Eye	58
Holiday	59
Meeting	60
Fewer Miracles	61
Learning to Count	64
Odd Jobs	65
The Father of Merchants	66
Aitaneet	68

Off the Map

We lived awhile
on the sunshine in photographs,
rebuilt on paper
              a town
whose street signs have all been taken down
and schoolyards sealed,
whose squares and lanes no longer tolerate
child's play:

Made maps
from which you could not be erased
though trees were felled and flags
burnt, tombs and monuments
levelled—
though armies marched from the south
                                      and east
and bolted the door of peace.

Body of clay huts
                and stone houses,
      Rainbow of clotheslines and sails,
                            Mother of travellers

Anything built on your chest throughout the ages
has been destroyed.
How often have we filled our pantries and cellars
to be looted, dug
for gold or drinking water
with only muscles to gain
and in the end, piped water in
from the next village.
                          It was our fig trees
and vineyards that withered; our apples
were the first eaten by worms.

Into strange cities you sent one family after the next
and waited for us to return
                              with medals
to pin on your chest.
No one recognized us; no one sent
back a postcard.
You lived on memories carved in rocks and caves.

On my map clouds still drift over the mountain, and slip
around the other side
to surface in lakewater. Birds
gabble from each roof
as the blind postman makes his tour.

On the Other Shore

When you open your eyes
it's sun rising over the lake, to set
   in fishing boats on the other shore.
Leaning close, I can even see
         the poor in Aitaneet, going to church,
awaiting miracles in God's lottery
and fishermen who work all day
         awaiting pickups by moonlight.

Laugh, and I hear them
    shouting to the drivers from their boats:
"Find me the prettiest one in your net, Salim!"
"That's for my wife—Second best
 for you, friend!"

Some wade in to shore
    for backslapping, and the fish
         are spirited away to cities.
Aitaneet hasn't the breasts to feed everyone
       (your plenty recalls that fact)

I follow you as you walk to your bedroom,
    you take off your dress,
        remove the bedcovers—
adjust the pillows.

In another city I see you crossing the street,
    police trailing you.

Made in Heaven

Night after night
Aunt Mary cooks vine leaves—
has never been known to dance with them
in her hair.

After supper the children must all be bathed
in a cement basin.
And she must be pregnant,

news for all the women in the neighbourhood
who'll gather to watch
a difficult birth.

She cries to heaven at each birth
or missed period,
yet obeys the priest:

Good to her husband, Aunt Mary is—
good to the neighbours,
with a recipe for all home remedies
but time.

Always a spare plate
and a kind word at her table
and for roving cats, an *auberge*
under the stove.

Aunt Mary spreads her affections like an endless
wash along a line
and she knits her sweaters
and mends her children's clothes

while night after night the farmers over the hill
latch their doors
light their kerosene lamps
and eat a solemn supper next to the woodstove.

Breach of Promise

Mister Nazim Hanna, now at peace
lived in the Catholic district
most of his life with his
mother, two cows, ten chickens and a cat.
He walked across town
around 1910, and brought back the wife
his elders had agreed on. He never could
remember the date, as the documents
had been lost, or burnt
when fire swept the altar
from an unwatched candle. Afterwards,
at any rate, they did everything
they were supposed to do.

Nazim Hanna paused in the fields
and wondered at the skies
when the rain would not come. He learned
to stake little on shepherds' predictions,
said only—"Enough over this year
to sell—God willing." Clouds
came and went with no rime or reason,
and the east wind never stayed
to wear out its welcome. But he kept
his end of the bargain.

In the middle of the First World War,
when bread had last been seen in the village
fourteen months before
and his wife gave birth to twin boys
and almost didn't survive the delivery
Nazim Hanna,
a strong man in his forties
went up on his roof, loaded his two-barrelled gun, and
shot God.

A Kiss

Seduced by words bigger
than any in my dialect,
and multifarious freedoms: the freedom to eat
indifferent food prepared at great expense
by strangers; freedom to loaf
in a bar; view films; make love
in parks; shave half my head
or grow a beard without
declaring a vocation for the priesthood . . . I tremble
to think of the freedoms my children will invent.

At Burger Bliss my young friend
disdains to eat the bun.
A slice of pickle whizzes past my ear
and slithers down the wall. No one
assumes the loss:
this generation is clearly marked for ruin.
My parents did not watch their intake
of sodium and carbohydrates
and I have to master the urge to tell an old-country tale
about the value of a piece of bread
during the war,
how granny and grandpa
still venerate crumbs—climaxed
with a linguistic lesson
that "bread" is the same word in our dialect
as "life."

Mine would scoff, but will my
children's children
also have reason to rescue each
morsel of bread that falls from the table
with a ritual kiss?

A Lullaby

No music, and the wind blows over the roofs.
    The children in Saint-Henri go to sleep
        hungry; no one
collects the garbage
    or cares for the gardens anymore.
Somewhere, rats
        keep vigil tonight
and the medical profession remains
        inflexible—"On strike."
Doctors ask for a thirty percent increase
    in salary. A crime
        is committed on Rosemount Boulevard
(police investigate)
King Cinyrasov visits
    the republic next door;
                the neighbours now
have all turned out the lights.

Catholic women must stop taking the pill.
    The Pope approves orgasm
only between married partners
and agrees with the king
    that communism and socialism are dead
(Nevertheless we are going
            on with the neutron bomb project)

Our child goes to sleep on my arm. Don't believe
all the newspapers say,
    stories can be told for no reason at all.
After I finish my tea
    we'll kiss goodnight
        and sleep as usual
(You must not read half the night,
    it's bad for the eyes).

A dog has ceased to bark in the basement. I check
the furnace room, everything is all right.

Come, rest your head on my pillow
     as sleep steals into your eyes.
          The world deteriorates
    from day to day, and we live our lives
among books and odd remarks.
Crimes and wars in the newspapers
          disturb us, of course
But tomorrow we'll go on as usual, serve dinner;
     I open the wine a bit too early.
                   Nasty, isn't it,
this business of killing all around us.
Some day we won't be here to tell the story.
    But what
          will bounce back
and go forth, and multiply?

Zero Hour

God struggles to show the world His face.
Tear down your barns—He is coming!
Should you have put up a curtain,
remove it.
Dismiss your ideas
and reconsider solutions.

Confess that
you did not love the hungry, really:
they brood too much.
That you knew no reason to dance for
dead issues, no reason
to play your pipes in the wilderness.
Loosing the seed in dark earth,
the swimmer in mad oceans—
evading or acknowledging the truth
was all the same.
God struggles to show the world His face.

He is coming! burn
your papers and notebooks.
Leave off the drinking bouts, and intimate nights;
liberate your wives and children;
don't wonder at the trees
discarding their leaves. Repeat:
I'll not cry again on a woman's shoulder
or utter profanities. Nor will I
debate with my friends.
I'll give up controversy.

Not in the Books

When the war came to Aitaneet
she was preparing for a wedding.

All the village feared
the world would be permanently deranged
and wondered what they had to do with it.

They hid their gold and wheat
so that if they had to die
no invader should have what was rightfully theirs.
They knew exactly what to do
once attacked,
and the memories of peace gradually faded.

They could not understand why their animals
                were apprehensive
and why the trees shed their leaves early
              during the war.
They wept and quarrelled with each other,
made up their differences, discussed freedom
and prayed to all the saints they could remember
while danger and fear grew daily more familiar—
food less so.
Whoever had any concealed it.

Young brides refused to sleep with their husbands.
Mothers prayed to die
before their children came to harm.
Their lives were small
and the earth was unkind . . .
                        Who, they asked, had
let this war slip
over their thresholds?

There was little sleep at nights
for thinking of the young men barricaded in ditches
who described their feelings afterwards.
They were told that God tries His servants—
and looked at each other and trembled.

Some died without a thought for heaven.
Some bled; lost limbs. Alive,
others sat and stared into space.

How could a little town above the lake resist?
All the war long Aitaneet
wept for her children.
Would history know of her saddened daughters,
                                   her living sons?
Will she enter the books?

And will the postponed wedding be rescheduled?

Enemy Ears

Pacing the valley,
    for the first few days
he made no kill. He pondered
    whether the task was practicable
and thought of trimming the ears
    from rabbits and foxes.

Once he broke off a branch
    and carved out the shape of a human ear.
He calculated that somewhere, someone
    was manufacturing plastic ears
which could be passed off for the real thing.

In dream, he harvested the valley
    of severed ears
which lay ripe to the hand: he dreamed
    the captain was elated
and ordered him to the fields again.

    Waking, he saw
a double-edged knife

with twenty-two notches
lying next to his head.

One Could Do Worse

In the middle of some nights
he'd lean his ladder against the tree
and quietly lop a few branches down

unearth the roots, lace them with acid
and hope that grass would soon spring up
 to cover his crime.

Then all summer he would sit on his steps
and wait for the first yellowed leaf to fall.
He'd call up the city (which had fathered it)
and ask permission to cut down the ailing tree.

Not one dog came to rub his flanks against the tree;
no one ever dreamed of suspending
a swing from its branches.
And year by year
the tree stood tall in its leaflessness
beside the whispering trees on the street,
a little gaunter than the year before
until the birds abandoned it altogether.

At last a city inspector
decided the tree was unsightly, a risk
to pedestrians.

Passing at midday I see a fine, white stump
                              in my neighbour's lawn.
The earth creeps up around it daily
and soon the snow will give it a decent burial.

Yet walking at dusk, I see the tree
alive and knowledgeable,
groping with perfect branches to complete
the order
              of trees on a street.

Through a Glass

Worms I see
in my dream, people who are like worms—
        crawling on the marble floor
away from the altar
        eying the Eucharist,
black flies on the windows,
        the fourteen stations
                missing.
I slip and find myself seated in the mud,
        searching for my resistance.
Skin'nbones,   kin'nbones.

Faces from the past turn about me:
        faces of the living,
                faces of the dead: weeping faces.
Others have strangled our symbols,
        taken our metaphors
                and told us lies.

Nuns and priests are stripping in the courtyard.
They stand, a moment, confused
        in the freedom of their genitals,
then fling their habits over their shoulders
and let fly at each other
        with fists and knees. Downstairs,
ladies with bare arms
        and high boots
        are asking for a stiff drink of whiskey
before they carry their dogs to bed.

Bold on the lonely street
        a girl stands
mixing tears with mascara,
waiting for a train to bring her man back

                          from the war.
But when the train comes
out crawl
              angleworm
                          caterpillar   spileworm
tapeworm   roundworm   army worm
                                      cankerworm   cutworm
         tobacco worm
worms from schoolyards and
                   out of used coffins
feeding on teabags and rotten shirts
                   pinworm   earthworm   tomato worm
twisting, pointing
              like dead trees on the mountain
                          woodworm   glowworm.

Someone's shot down at the door.
                                 Skin'nbones.
Here come all the trucks
              of the world, loaded with machine guns
for export to the East.
The wheels of the trucks squeal in chorus,
              the drivers lower their heads
                   and cross horns.

What's this? The aged bridegroom
                   creeps up the aisle,
his bride in a scarlet dress.
Later they drop by the morgue
to burn all their pens and pencils.

I wake up
         go back to sleep
see tree roots bursting out of rocks,
              clouds packed inside my linen chest
                   and water pouring from my books.

My hand closes on someone's pillow,
                now a mound of bones.

Women and men ride
                elevators and I with them.
A strange smell fills the air and I smile,
                refusing to explain myself.

Hair thins out on top of my head
                and shoots from ears and nose,
my aborted child cries to me
                from the abortionist's lab,
                I am finally sharing and contributing
                      to the human ordeal.
I convince you that a visit to the doctor
                is the best solution under the circumstances,
                and in my dream
I see you lying on the table bleeding.

Ben Hilali's Night of Revels

He comes
out of the bar holding onto his senses,
splinters of the evening
wedged in his head. Even the lampposts
misted over, appear to be ladies
                    pressing close
to fill his glass: emptying theirs
into artificial flowerpots. He, feeling generous,
asks, "Who's the greatest lover on this block?"
(How'll I ever get home—if I have one?)
and orders another round. "On me, thankoo ver'much."

Flounders on a quarter-block considering
what his wife will say when he does,
how the kids will eye him.
Tell them: "I met God in the street,
hitching a lift in a three-piece suit!
His chin was shaved, and He looked
less conspicuous. Said He'd come down
to see how His people were doing."

He rests his head against a wall
blotched with the contents
of exhaust pipes and spray cans. Wonders
at the subtemperatures
stone can resist.
"So I say, 'Listen, I lost my job
and my house. My wife and kids hate me.' And He looks
up and down the street and sighs, 'My, the place
has certainly changed.'
'No takers?' I ask.
'Time was,' says He, 'I only had to
lift a finger . . . '
                        I tell Him

the bus service around here is reliable
and He doesn't leave me empty-handed.
Sells me a lottery ticket."

Always loved stones—marvelled at their composition.
How they scatter in fields,
come to attention
in bridges. Would like to find out:
are there any in heaven?
Would love to achieve a state of solidity
resting on a mountain
under a snowdrift
bottom of the lake
brushing cheeks with fish
keeping time with the undercurrent
knowing, for a moment, that something is happening to me.

       —Yet being homeless
is not so bad. My dears, all of us are promised
a place in heaven. Barring that, a tin cup
and a spot for the rump
on the banks of the Euphrates.
Ji'tu ila Baghdada—
 I came to Baghdad
 in the palm leaves and river water,
 in the lungs of a bird . . .
Bummed a lift, of course.
 And I saw Abu Nuwas letting everyone in
 as he babbled and clutched at the bottle
      of chemistry.

The lines were coming! He'd not have to strain
to recite three hundred, if asked.
 One day poems will walk through the gate
      of the city
 toward the land of—
land of something or other.

> *And estrangement will become the land of*
> *the prophets;*
> *One day stars will walk on earth like women.*
One day men will walk on earth
like men.
He'd take on any Arab
and drive home any point. But no one asks.

Lovers of poetry; persecutors
of poets! He dips
into the delicious shadows
to relieve himself: grins, when a brother reveller
speaks to him, the lilting voice
of Abu Nuwas.

It is a glorious hour, my boy. Nothing
should interfere with your thoughts. No one tell you
how to screw your head on
or the world up; how to make a more regular
contribution to the foul-up.
So they wish to engage in warfare?
Let them do so. They'll finish each other off
one way or another, soon enough.

Now who will arise
and listen to us, Brother Nuwas?

He finds his feet and shuffles on,
tongue curled on his lip
to taste the aromas of the city. A boy and girl
overtake him on a motorcycle and one yells
"Go home, you drunken nut!"
He is not responsible for their manners
and goes on hunting for
the vanished shadows,
careful of his limbs. What's left of the city
begins to buzz in his ears. Absurd

to make much of it, the perilous journey
with the reward at the end.
No more than a meeting
in the dark between hungry bodies,
with seventy years of trying to understand what happened—
name left in a notebook.
Absurd, this fuss
over names
when all know how short is
the time given to wear them. Leave them like markers
in your place.
The book will never be picked up again.

Under his breath he tries on names:
Abu Nuwas Ali Ben Abi Talib.
Abd al-Rahman al-Dakhil, The Hawk of Quraysh.
Shadi Ben Hilali. This is my name, and not
a great one: only a hat
that a gust of God would steal from my ears.
Vain to hold onto it,
as I do; still worse
to cry over the wrecks
of our grandfathers' hats.

Kids! Your Grandpa refused to be buried
or cremated. Donated his bones
to rebuild Granada
and Baghdad, Damascus
or Jerusalem
upon the sands of rhetoric.
He lied through the puffs from his pipe
and the swish of his rocking-chair,
lied in his jokes and prayers
and memories.
Ours is the greatest
nation on earth.
(I was an oak, now I am a willow, I can
bend . . .)

Only Niha and Mount Herman are eternal.
Children, remember
the graves of your grandfathers:
there is nothing in the past
to scream for.

A woman rounds the corner and
picks up speed, worries
planted on her face
and recently watered. He hollers, "Stop and listen
to my latest anecdote! I've given up composing
music, dear, it doesn't pay
but I'd sell my history to an eclipsed moon
to buy some shimmer for your hair. Open your heart,
my love, let me be buried there. Cover
my shame with a paper napkin.
Place a block-heater on my grave!"

A woman is a passing thing.
Now there is only a toad
crossing his path. He spits in anger,
wipes his chin with the back of his hand.
How he longs to be
in a cathedral or a mosque
and assure God that he is still alive.
But all the doors in the city
have locked him out.
A man should be able to have a word with God
                                at any time.
Looking up, he finds the old man
has slipped out and is
preoccupied with billiards—shooting stars
across the sky.
He calls one Adonis
and wonders if it would make a good home.
Ya, Nuwasi, how is it that a poet
on the shores of the Mediterranean

can never find a home, yet knows
all the jails in the East?

Little sister, write me about
how the geese travel in winter. What kind of mileage
we make. All those posters
in Martyr Square: Whatever became of them?
Tell me about
the palmtrees, do they still spit dates?
I understand the cobbles have almost been
denuded of rubble. Write and tell me,
my dear, what you did
when they came to rape the women
and filch your flowerpots? It must have been
a sight: Beirut
tumbling into the sea
without an earthquake.

"Look at my dress," she says, "does it
make me elegant?"
She'd bought it yesterday
half-price. On that account his sins will be reduced
by fifty percent on the day of judgment. His bones
will be exhibited in a museum: Ben Hilali,
a gleaming fossil in a showcase,
the knuckles of his right hand over his pelvic bone.
He himself will write the legend:
"On the day I was born the sun did not rise
but all the trees bowed.
Their branches and leaves went looking for water."
He would have to change his dirty shirt,
or wrap himself in tissue. As well
spread a tree around his nakedness, or beg to change
the course of his life.
He sees his wife
naked, waiting in bed.
Odd that the stairs he climbs

and the door he knocks on are not his,
and the woman in his arms
is wearing a nightgown.
He tells her to put a brassière on—
"It excites me"—confesses
that he was sure he was going to die
the year before, but didn't,
and is amazed that dirty thoughts
can survive in such a clean room.
"I am a computer, and you are
the terminal!"
                        Birds sing inside his head,
find nests in his ideas.
Remember all those women who cried
and wiped their tears on their husbands' shirts?
refused to surrender
when the city fell?
In the end they, too, had to give up
and be turned into a movie.

People spoke of how apple trees
were blasted upside down. Nothing was said
about the men
under the debris.

He feels for the notebook
in his pants, and writes:
> I know everything.
> I don't have to go home.
> God will wait.
> I am fluent in love and in the consumption
> of beer. Things I Need to Do Tomorrow:
> Nothing

but Collect Beer Cans
        and Brandy Cigars.
These words will be preserved

in his breast pocket, against the erosion
of his intellectual output.
Let others mourn the dead cells
of their brains, and every parting hair;
speak of the madness of God who carries
whips in both hands;
compose last songs
or an epigram to be remembered by.
(The heels of hope spurred on my blood . . .   Hope,
burning like an endless cigarette in my mouth . . .)
Half-naked, he hangs out the window
and finds the night pleading for his return.
"Mr. Shadi Ben Hilali accepts with pleasure . . . "

Outside his woman's apartment
a crane is arrested in the sky.
He straddles the fence at the edge of the lot
and waves his hands up
and down, like a maestro
directing his orchestra.

This is the newest building in town! Come on
boys, let's get it up. A little elbow grease
goes a long way. Out of your beds
and man that crane!—to the tractors! Which of you
is worthy of his spade and helmet?

Once the face of a worker on a construction site
was plain to me. Now it is
the face of Adonis.
Come all you workers, cover this age
with your warm bodies and beating breasts!
Bye and bye
we shall drink to another.

A Native Son Remembers Us in His Will

Lord, do not absent Yourself
from the world of men: this inconvenience
is only temporary.
Now where shall we place the altar
and the doors? We'll have to ship in
white stone from the North, yellow sand
from the city—
cement and iron from the next town.
The Catholic priest will let us use
his church in a pinch. (For a long time
he's had his eye on our bell.)
We'll bring in candles
and altarcloths, and have the confessional
installed; pass the plate twice on Sundays
and be reminded about the widow's mite.
After mass, we'll stroll along
to see how the work's progressing.

But supposing the money runs out
halfway up the walls? What if
the mayor embezzles it?
Send the priest on a fund-raising tour
to America.
But masses would be postponed in his absence
and You Yourself, Lord, might leave town,
seeing that Your old home's torn down
and the new one not ready yet.
You, Lord, might go up the mountain, build Yourself
a shack, and live there all alone.
We should have to send a delegation.
It is no laughing matter
for half-a-dozen of our elders
to pant up the flank of a mountain
hoping to entice You back,

and possibly be refused
an audience. Look, supposing that priest
swindles us too? Lord, do not
absent Yourself from the world of men.

Inventory

At the crack of dawn she wakes up
        throws the covers aside
        straightens pillows, passes fingers
        through her tangled hair

                barefoot, walks to her dresser
                and faces the mirror
                      observing every detail.

The face is still the same
the eyes, nose, mouth
        the cheekbones
                the forehead, and the chin
                all the same
        the shoulders, breasts
                and neck
        stomach, pubic hair
        and thighs
                all the same.

At the crack of dawn
        she smashes the mirror with her fist
                and watches the blood
                      trickle down her arm.

In Suspense

Wedged between two swwandbags
like fat ladies on a bus,
the back of his head
developed blisters.

Told not to move
he played with his springy hair
and waited for his moustache to grow.

Dreaming of the mulberry tree and
churchyard in his village,
of a girl his own age about to undress,

and calling to mind the bell tower proud
                   above the church
and how the snow looked,

or sitting up late gaming
with God, bribing the angels,
talking like an old widow, chattering
about the war,
X-rated movies and
love for mankind,
of her eyes and thin nightgown windblown
from the clothesline which bared
the secrets of her house,

blocking his nose to the hospital smells
(messages from dead children),

touching himself whenever the nurse left the room,
asking

—how has the rain been this year on the mountain?

and the goat our Dad was raising,
has she borne any young?

So they burnt a flag and two trees
in the street one day . . .
—do guys still stand idle in the square
and look at her legs when she passes by?

An Umbrella

I try to recall what it is to be calm
with the noise of traffic outside your window
not in my ears.
A door closes in the distance
and I think of another in your bed
twisting your hair round your neck,
kissing away tears
and telling you lies:

Sure that some overwhelming, mysterious guilt
lives in your head, that you think
everything is either/or
and your eyes signal for the love of a man.

Or say that I have been
awakened from my sleep by a nightmare,
got up, walked to my kitchen,
had a glass of milk
and gone back to sleep.

A detective stands outside your door,
    the rain splutters on the windowsill.

        Give the man an umbrella
and turn your doubts loose again.

The Cocktail Hour

He would dial his friends' numbers
and hang up before the phone rang,
mix a drink, and watch the ice melt in the glass—
select a card from his fan of stray beginnings
and invent the rules for proceeding
toward a satisfactory end.
The risk was in being overmatched by an idea:
having to drop it, and take up a new one.

He would comfort himself by thinking that
in the great wide city
some other human being like him
or unlike him
must be watching the melting ice
in an untouchable glass,
the desire to cry or laugh having deserted him
and the silence around him not a choice of his own.

Or be visited by the madness or compulsion that
leads a person sitting behind a desk
to undertake ordering the nature of things.
Someone else would be going through a dictionary
looking for unfamiliar words and their origins.

Innocent Pursuits

Sometimes he saw nothing in Aitaneet
but a blackbird preening its wings
on a utility pole

and what's this love of a town
that sleeps and wakes to the pecking of birds?
He'd no time to be timid or moral
yet the plum tree before his house never
forgot to blossom on time.

He followed the girls from one end of Aitaneet
to the next—
generally, they ran away.

Girls his own age changed overnight,
began to wear dresses and be mindful of their hair.
And what use to play with those
respecters of fences? He, and a few boys, reigned
in the alleys,
chasing mating cats and looking
in windows for bathing women,
watching the older girls hang clothes out on the line
while water trickled down
their blouses.

They raided barns and stole eggs
to exchange the next day for ice-cream,
chuckling about a farmer
so close-fisted that he pocketed
the blessing in church
so as not to pass it on;
and about his wife, who sent marauding

roosters from her kitchen
with tailfeathers through their combs.

Nights, they'd slip out of bed
for a rendezvous
under old Mansour's open windows
to interrupt his snoring
with imitations, or the application of cold water:
later, creep back
to see if his ardour
had also been awakened.

In their hilarious courts they passed
judgment on every adult in town:

On the schoolmaster
in his one presentable jacket,
who thoughtfully picked his nose
and entered the classroom by the window.

On the black-browed priest
who stood them against the wall
one-legged, the whole afternoon
for slips in catechism,
but was a pushover
in the confessional.

And on beautiful Miriam, huge-breasted Miriam
alone in her house at the edge of town
entertaining a few men—
not all at once—in the evening.
They'd offer to help her pick olives
but remained on the ground
while she tugged at her skirts
in the treetops.

During the week they rested their consciences
                                  up for Sunday
when they'd have to file a report on their sins.
But what meant a *mea culpa* to them
if lambs and kids
were on parade
and the plum trees staged a spectacular
show each spring?

The girls kept him busy.

They skimmed over the snow in winter
and laughed with their friends behind trees in summer
playing their own incomprehensible games,
tossing their useless hair.

And he wrote verses,
offering them to the snow.

Ancestral Voices

Saeed bin al-Asi:
"He who does not write,
his right hand is
as useless as his left."
Man ibn Zaydah:
"The hand that does not write
is as useless as a leg."
Al-Zubayr bin Bakkar:
"Writers are kings
and the rest, animal drivers."
Al-Muqaffa:
"Mankind needs writers
more than writers need kings."
Anonymous:
"He who writes does not fear mortality."

We Have Some Sight Left

We must be the only ones
                        left in Aitaneet:
three old men
        sitting in the square
                rolling our worrybeads in our fingers
in the midst of a memory contest.
One speaks of the war,
        another of his dead wife,
                and I speak of the deserted
                          streets in the empty town.

The wind twirls discarded newspapers,
        dust mounts on windowsills
                and no bridal dough dries
                      over the doorframes.
All the young men are gone—
        some to their graves,
                others to a far-away land
from which come letters
                      and some money to live on.
Some there are who will never be heard from.
Young women spend
        their days expectant
                and their nights in hostile, lonely beds.
They too
        will leave in the end
                to join
                the young men and build
                        a new Aitaneet elsewhere.

What shall we do
                with the remaining years,
                we who are empty wardrobes,
                      with our thinning bones?

Those of us
    who have some sight left
        do not see children
            playing in the alleys.
Those with a little breath sing:
   The gold in September's leaves
     under the windows
         brings you to me
      as pictures cannot.
Those who hear a little
    wonder: how many sleeping pills
would silence
           the crickets at night?
Alive, yet aware of death,
    we've made and destroyed
       our own legend.
Once we filed complaint against a storm,
    cast fishhooks at a cloud
        when the larders ran low.
How will we lease our days,
    we the broken clocks
       and dry fountains,
           the defaced street signs?
And will the nights grow longer anyway?

None of us has ever crossed the ocean
       or left Aitaneet,
only read old books and
      interpreted the language
        for our children.
The coming years could erase these words
   and our descendants (boy
    home from war
       with half a face; girl seated
        before the mirror
     adjusting a strand of fate—)

Our flesh holds no surprises
        and the skin is subject to cracks
                            and bruises
    But still we love our women
            and appease them, as the saying goes.

If time waits for prisoners
            to come home in poems,
urges all travellers
            to return to their native land
and begs the martyrs to retreat
            from remote ideas,
let time implore Aitaneet
                    to forgive us our indecision!
Which of us has loved and worshipped
            his woman
worn her nakedness, held her
                    to his chest
and felt the rush of her
            blood in his?
Which of us has disinterred
            his history
                and exposed its lies?
The past has not kept us wondering
        how to sustain this dream. The origin
            of a small town on a hill
            did not concern us.
Would any now
    face death to defend
            what he cannot explain?

Every extra day of life in the square is a bonus.
We still walk
    the streets of the village
expecting to meet
                our own shadows,
    which we greet

and measure for consistency
                    against our dreams.
Had our poems been truer than our aim,
            higher than the houses,
no invader might have erased the lines
        or burned down the library!
With fatigue and deliberate ease we avoid
        certain parts of town
                the new Turks have taken. We sigh:
This war has changed her face.
Will she be theirs in the end
        to care for, or reduce
                        to rubble?
Why did we ever
build her houses
            and blast her trees into bloom?

Cruel to force her breath again
in a poem or song. Leave me a memory, she cries,
                unrecorded, untouched!
Your right hand has
        uncovered my gold,
your left released
        my waters.
By night you still spin me into fables
            and hide me in dreams.
I had no enemies,
        or so I thought—
Like love
        I never counted
            strokes and caresses,
Like love
        I opened my heart
            to the hurt and joy.
My hands are empty, now: will you
    love me still
            or hold back?

Take from me
>> sunlight,
> smooth as the wind,
>> gentle as water
> and real as my streets.
Take from me
> reason in a new year,
>> and solve your feuds.

The child has gone.
Suspended over the water
> on the hilltop
she carries a school bag
>> into a deserted school yard,
>> and those who bore her
>>> cannot take care of her.
Between one nap and the next
> her features age
and if death would come in a snooze
> as it will one day,
it would only be a longer nap,
> Aitaneet a home for shadows
>> and the lake
>>> a flash behind the eyes.

None of us
> rings her church bell any longer,
>> none carries a pitcher to water her trees.
Who will, in the end,
> carry our coffins
>> to the grave?

R.I.P.

However many
        ways you can discuss
                a nuclear missile
you cannot outwit one

Regardless of
        editorials and poems that play
            back the horrors
                of war, the war
        will always be
            more horrible

Whatever words are employed
        to describe death, the most
            effective are still
                Rest in Peace.

The Contortionist

You come to me when the years have begun
to etch
    plans for a new world
                on forehead and cheeks,
    when my loins have
           acquired a new intelligence and
    my blood will not
      storm as readily.
How shall I marshall
            the fireflies aswarm in my head,
            flitting everywhere?
How break down
            the desires before they are desires?
I can twist my back
    into a rainbow, or let the lines
        fall flat on the page—
Ignore the mouth,
            the touch on the arm,
                the tap on the shoulder.

Have I the patience, the alchemy
        to make days of nights,
                nights of days?

Propel me
    back to my history
        and my fears.

Words

The colours of words must be sensed
              before their size enters the eye
or layout penetrates the mind
We smell their
         flowers
taste them
              and chew on their leaves and twigs
We hear them—notes
         of past and recent history
                  enticing our ears to displace other sounds
We break them into pieces
         and   s
                    c
                    a
                    t
                    t
                    e
                    r
                              them
                              over
                              our
                              skins
to feel their edges and textures

but when we try to capture them
they shy away
        to some unreachable region
            in the brain

One Fish

You need obtain only two things:
a keyboard
and enough blank paper. Any interest
in mythology and legends,
put to rest. Read history,
and think about the fate of nations. Become
like the town idiot
commissioned by his sister to bring home a fish—
too late for market,
holding your basket under the mouth
of a gargoyle that spews
rainwater from the rooftop
crying, "Please, God,
one fish!"

You do not want a wife to go shopping with,
or a child to interrupt your nightmares.
Humanity, as such, need not concern you.
Developments
political and economic
are not a part of your world.
Conventions could take place
daily on your front lawn; committees
could study peace on earth
and render their recommendations;
but you would not even be tempted
to see the published results.

You will be caught up in the riddle
of the immediate present. Three
or two, or one meal a day would suffice.
The necessity
of washing your face and taking a shower
may present a problem. But robots

will soon direct
dirty clothes into the washer
and return them to the closet.
You may switch off the telephone,
cover the T.V.
with a rag, and resolve not to listen
to the news on the radio
So that you can lie on your bed, walk
up and down the room
or sit behind the desk and await inspiration.

Fortunes

No gods go walking here
yet some claim to have heard them
creeping out of caves
at night, clearing mines and barricades
to drop a blessing,
starting like wild creatures at the first sounds
    of war.

No gods go walking here
yet the mountain bends down to listen
    to fortune-tellers.
One family lives in a paper bag,
    another under a tin sheet
and they buy their meat at empty counters,
shelter in some roofless church,
    peel apples
        on the sidewalk.

All the Lights

His watch stops
        four hours into
a permanent sleep.

His child, his house, and his city
              no longer appeal to him,
                  no longer retain him.

A dandy in his dark suit
      careless of the passages that he will not re-read,
      of the lovers outgrown,
            of grandchild unseen—
His books, his records and his desk
    no longer appeal to him,
    no longer retain him.
With what regrets? what sense of sin
                    or grace?
He leaves
    with all the lights on.

The Eye

Every other village in the valley
boasted an eye: Bear's Eye,
Deer's Eye
Eyes of Roosters, Scorpions
Figs and Butter—

But the ground would not wink for us
when we leaned on our spades, listening
for the tremor of water.

Holiday

If they ventured upon roads disguised by snow
it was to rush out, bury
their faces in it,
blaze trails on the whitened ground.
Everyone waited for the snow to fall
except old ladies and foreigners.
It descended on the village
like a temporary lunacy.

They made men and weapons of snow, built
and destroyed houses and caves,
rushed inside
to display the flakes on their hair and eyebrows
and when they thought they were cold,
burnt wood in the old stove
and sat talking about the snow,
drinking tea by the fire
for nobody went to work when the snow fell.

Snowbirds came to the attic and slept
through it all, later
took their young and travelled on.

He dreamt of buying a suit and a tie,
of building a house on a hill
and living in a land where the
snow falls daily, waited
                     for a sleigh to steal him away

Meeting

Lodged in you
    like a friendly secret—
held
    like a certainty
        in the mind.

This is nothing mysterious;
   two mere human beings,
statistics rattle at our windows.
But we come together and
     for a few moments get the better
        of them, as one.

Shadows have not yet claimed our eyes
  nor the sheets slipped from our shoulders.

Fewer Miracles

In Aitaneet bells call the order of morning and evening.
The west wind swoops down from the mountain
and the farmers wait for something to happen.
Old Hassan lumbers out of his grocery shop
and takes down a decayed Coca Cola sign.

Children skip and shriek in the alleys,
dust curtains the figures in windows
while in each front yard a woman
bends stiffly over a tub
and the smell of cut wheat breezes into town.

Here no affair
is a seven-day wonder. Over tubs and pipes
it is still avowed
that a Turk shot their bell
in the First World War, miffed
by the din it made
and marvelled that, since the Turks left
the bell rings truer than ever.

Now many wars and fewer miracles later, Old Hassan
swears as the rusty nails that held the sign break.
During the day a very few customers
visit his shop, and in between
he hears the news drumming on the transistor radio,
every once in a while
hitching up his suspenders.
The only time he closes shop
is Sunday mornings, or when a funeral
is passing by. He lunches discreetly
behind the counter, beams

when one of his daughters drops in,
rinses his hands in cold water
and plays backgammon in the afternoons.

Old Hassan sells salt and sugar
and sunflower seeds;
Old Hassan sells tobacco and fruit
and hands out cold remedies for free;
and Old Hassan stands guard over the sweets counter
but is easily taken in.
He doesn't mind giving credit,
yet religiously believes
that the cash register should ring in
the first sale of the day.

Old Hassan knows nothing about eternity
though his imagination is robust.
He gathers his wits like a lost dream
and tells his friends stories
when they come to buy bread in the evening.
He knows of a mountain lion
so fierce it could sever a horse's head
in two bites,
and so nimble, it could toss
that head up in the air,
bound onto the ledge
of its den, high on the rock-face
of the mountain
and catch the snack before it fell again.

Old Hassan tells how men carried two hundred
kilo stone slabs on their backs
to build the old bridge, now standing
beneath fathoms of water
since the government erected a dam.
And how the architect himself laid coins
in each layer

to distract the evil spirits that would
flock to pull it down.

He doesn't believe that winter's the bad season,
nor that the world will come to an end,
and Old Hassan expounds his political theories
as he sees fit. The day the bells cease to ring
                                        in Aitaneet
Old Hassan swears he'll close shop and leave town.

Learning to Count

Years change swiftly now
    and are less tractable.
The world still spins to shadowbox with cares.
    Love alone, they say, sustains us
—but love drifts in all directions,
    an officious wind
taking the leaves of trees from place to place.

Out of my chest, out of my hand
    one poem tumbles
and it is doubtful that any wonders will.
    Only half
my fears and doubts have been realized
    yet the other half cling to my skin
like leeches. I cover my age
    with rags and inquiries.

As a child I counted animals,
    sometimes stars; in my teens,
only the hours and the minutes;
    in my twenties, days and weeks.
Next it was months and years. Now
    I'm looking at decades and centuries.
Shall I learn to count eternities?

Odd Jobs

At sunset he pauses in the middle of the back yard.
The apple tree reclines against the fence,
slow to recover
in splints and bandages.
There's a crack in the wall of the house
and another in the balcony woodwork
beyond the skill of his hammer.
Neither can he renew
a country half-destroyed,
a continent edging to the sea,
a city
sleeping on its crimes.

Nevertheless, he rakes up leaves
and she binds the rosebush.
Autumn is early this year. The weed
in the grass has died; some seasonal plants
are still alive.
The shrubs are trimmed,
the grass mowed,
and the storm windows are all in place.
The children have locked the kitchen door.

Sunset catches them in the middle
of the back yard.
There is nothing left to do. This day
is almost over.

The Father of Merchants

He leans against my wall, a red face
in a silver-rimmed frame
arrested by his tie:
an old man proud of white hair and moustache
and the years ploughing forehead and cheeks
now that he, too, has thankfully
laid down the plough and scythe.
                    From the smile
tamed by the picture you would not suspect
that he was a master-joker—at weddings, had them
rolling in the aisles.
He must have given in to the occasion with a sly chuckle
and made the photographer ruin half
a roll of film, before he'd hold
the correct pose for ten seconds running,
and not cause the thumb
to slip while the belly shook.

Only his picture
in twenty-odd living rooms
made it to this continent. He dreamed
of becoming a father
of merchants, and every year dispatched
a son or daughter to America
by mortgaging another parcel of good farmland

until grandma alone was left to hear out his jokes,
and she much preferred to have a letter
from America read aloud
while mending socks of an evening
in the kitchen.

One spring he surprised her over her elbows
in a tub of flour, while on the counter

rose mountain ranges of the Easter cakes
her children and grandchildren loved. Staring,
he trumpeted, "Who do you imagine
will eat these, old woman?"
                    She rubbed
a little dough in her eyes, and sighed.
"I've baked my pastries every blessed Easter.
God knows old habits die hard."
"You planning to send 'em
Special Delivery to America?"

She reapplied herself to patting cakes, humming
no more seasonal melodies
while the old man stalked off in search of the
                    family album.

He shook out a picture for each
place at the broad table,
and plied the smiling faces with fresh cakes.
"C'mon now," he coaxed, pressing the pastries
closer to each dear one. "Eat for grandpa,
sweetheart, eat!"

with a bullet hole in the middle of it,
and the kids poking about the streets
with schoolbags and runny noses
—sometimes caught crouching
in homemade undershorts
stamped with the brand of flour
used by their families.
     And the minor commotion
caused when, every once in a while, a car
enters and leaves the town,
with nothing but a cloud of dust behind it.

I'd like to forget that the doctor visited
only once a week
and set up clinic in the deserted room
over the grocery shop: how ingrown toenails
were scraped and pulled out
with pliers.
    Yet, having no anaesthetic
he talked of the lost
    city of caves
crowning the hilltop half a mile from home,
far from any
apparent source of water;
said to conceal a tunnel through the heart
of the hill to the river
in the valley below,
beside the fabled wealth of a Phoenician queen.
He told me that wealth
was in the undeciphered writing
on walls of mountain caverns
    where I played:
not where men scraped in the dust on moonless
nights, muffling the sounds
of their quest behind slabs
of wood.
    Perhaps forgetfulness is a luxury

I can do without.
There's danger in emptying too many thoughts,
or not thinking at all . . . danger
of hours
passing by without faces; of not
noticing when it's noon
          or knowing that
sudden shadows would be making
men of the boys,
though the sun would soon snatch them away
leaving the dried figs sticky in pockets
of clamberers to caves.

Sun over the mountain . . .